P9-DNL-955

Trucks
Inside and Out

Chris Oxlade

PowerKiDS press

New York

Published in 2009 by The Rosen Publishing Group Inc.
29 East 21st Street, New York, NY 10010

Copyright © 2009 Wayland/The Rosen Publishing Group, Inc.

All rights reserved. No part of this book may be reproduced in any
form without permission from the publisher, except by a reviewer.

First Edition

Senior Editor: Jennifer Schofield
Editor: Rob Scott Colson
Designer: Darren Jordan
Consultant: Ben Russell

Library of Congress Cataloging-in-Publication Data

Oxlade, Chris.
    Trucks inside and out / Chris Oxlade. — 1st ed.
        p. cm. — (Machines inside out)
    Includes index.
    ISBN 978-1-4358-2862-9 (library binding)
    ISBN 978-1-4358-2940-4 (paperback)
    ISBN 978-1-4358-2944-2 (6-pack)
    1. Trucks—Parts—Juvenile literature. 2. Trucks—Equipment and supplies—Juvenile literature.
    3. Trucks—Juvenile literature. I. Title.
    TL230.15.09525 2009
    629.224--dc22

                              2008025729

Manufactured in China

Acknowledgments
Cover Fernando Rodrigues/Dreamstime.com
6 John Van Straalen, 7t General Motors, 7b John Van Straalen, 8–9 Kevin Hulsey Illustration, Inc., 8 Paula
Gent/Dreamstime.com, 9 Max Blain/Dreamstime.com, 10–11 Kevin Hulsey Illustration, Inc., 12t Zoediak/Dreamstime.com,
12b Paul A. Souders/CORBIS, 13 H. Kent Sundling/MrTruck.net, 14–15 Dannyphoto80/Dreamstime.com, 15 H. Kent
Sundling/MrTruck.net, 16–17 Chrysler LLC. Dodge (the Dodge Ram's Head Logo are trademarks of Chrysler LLC),
16 Nick Stubbs/Dreamstime.com, 17 H. Kent Sundling/MrTruck.net, 18 John Van Straalen, 19t David Freund/istockphoto,
19b Dreamstime.com, 20t Chris Scotti, 20b Stahlkocher/Wikipedia GNU, 21 Kevin Hulsey Illustration, Inc., 22 Jolin/
Dreamstime.com, 23b Michael Emerson/Dreamstime.com, 23t David Monniaux/Creative Commons ShareAlike,
24 Walter Hodges/Brand X/Corbis, 25t John Van Straalen, 25b Frederic Pitchal/Sygma/Corbis, 26 Jack
Mills/Dreamstime.com, 27b Elementalimaging/Dreamstime.com, 27t Thomas Mounsey/istockphoto

Contents

A truck is a complicated machine. Inside a truck, there are thousands of parts, from the heavy metal engine block, to delicate electronic components that work the driver's instrument panel. This book explains how trucks work. It looks at large cargo trucks, such as the Peterbilt truck below, and smaller pickup trucks, such as the Isuzu on page 8.

Driver's cab

Diesel engine

Radiator

Tractors and trailers

Trucks come in many shapes and sizes. The truck on these pages is called a tractor unit. Its job is to pull trailers, which are connected at the back. The tractor unit and trailer together are called an articulated truck.

Tractor unit

Trailer

Right-hand drive

For the United Kingdom and Australia, trucks are built with the steering wheel on the right-hand side of the car, like this one. For the United States and most countries, the steering wheel is on the left. Other parts are in the same place.

TECH FACT

The largest trucks in the world are in Australia. They are called road trains, because one tractor unit pulls up to four trailers, in the same way that a train locomotive pulls several cars. The heaviest road trains weigh almost 200 tons (the same weight as 300 elephants).

Fuel tank

Engine compartment cover

Wheels

Truck structure

A truck needs a super-strong structure to support its weight and the weight of the cargo it carries. The main structure is called the chassis (say SHA-SEE). The chassis is a steel frame under the truck's body, which stretches from the front to the back. All the other parts of the truck are attached to the chassis.

Body

Rails and crossmembers

The chassis has two long pieces of steel called rails. There is one rail on each side of the truck. These are joined together by shorter pieces of steel, called crossmembers. There are holes in the rails and crossmembers for other parts to be bolted onto the chassis.

The fifth wheel

The tractor unit of an articulated truck has a connector on the back of its chassis. The connector is known as the fifth wheel. A large pin on the trailer slots into the fifth wheel. It locks into place so that the tractor can pull the trailer.

Fifth wheel

Trailer structure

The trailer of an articulated truck also has a chassis. Two long rails run from front to back, joined together by crossmembers. They support the weight of the cargo in the trailer. The wheels, legs, and body of the trailer are attached to the chassis.

TECH FACT

A chassis is carefully designed to take the weight of the truck and its cargo. The rails and crossmembers inside a big cargo truck are wider, deeper, and made of thicker steel than those in a pickup truck. The larger chassis is stronger and stiffer, so it does not bend under the load.

Engine

I-TEC

Rail

Crossmember

Wheels and suspension

A truck's wheels spread its weight over the road. Two or four wheels are turned by the engine. Tires grip the road so that the truck can turn corners, accelerate, and brake safely. Suspension allows the wheels to move up and down as the truck goes over bumps. The suspension keeps the tires in contact with the road and stops the truck from bouncing up and down.

Shocks and springs

Each wheel is attached to the chassis by an arm that lets it move up and down. Springs on each arm support the chassis. Each wheel also has a shock absorber, which stops the spring from becoming too squashed if the truck hits a large bump.

Shock absorber

Air suspension

Many trucks have air suspension. In these trucks, each wheel is attached to a rubber bag. The rubber bag is effectively a very strong balloon, and works just like a spring. The pressure of the air inside the bag can be adjusted to raise or lower the suspension.

TECH FACT

Tires are filled with air. The air pressure must be just right to stop the tires from wearing out unevenly. Too much air and the center of the tread wears down. Too little, and the outsides of the tread wear down. Uneven wear can make a tire burst or the truck skid in wet weather.

Spring

Shock absorber

-TEC

Truck tires

A truck's tires are made from rubber strengthened inside with thin layers of steel. Truck tires are larger and stronger than car tires, because they must carry much more weight. The tire tread pushes water away, letting the tire grip a wet road.

Tire

Wheel

Truck engines

Trucks need powerful engines to get moving and to pull heavy cargoes. Most trucks have diesel engines. These engines are more efficient and more powerful than gasoline engines. But they are heavier. The fuel burns inside spaces called cylinders. The burning fuel pushes pistons along the cylinders. This movement turns the engine's crankshaft.

Engine arrangements
The engine on the opposite page is called an in-line six, because it has six cylinders arranged in a straight line. This is the most common type of diesel truck engine, but smaller trucks may have

Under the hood
A truck's engine is often in front of and below the driver's cab, under the hood. The engine is attached to the front part of the chassis. On cabover trucks, the whole cab tips forward to let an engineer work on the engine.

Lubrication
The metal parts of a truck engine are constantly moving against each other. Engine oil allows them to move without rubbing and wearing out. This is called lubrication. The oil is pumped around by an oil pump, and kept clean by oil filters like these shown above.

Flywheel

Piston

Cylinder

Connecting rod

Crankshaft

TECH FACT

Truck engines are larger, heavier, and far more powerful than car engines. A truck engine can weigh over a ton (heavier than a whole family car). The largest engines have a capacity of up to 4.23 gallons (16 liters)— 10 times that of a 54 oz. (1.6-l) car engine. They produce 10 times the power, too.

How the engine works

As a diesel engine runs, each cylinder follows a sequence of moves. This sequence is called the four-stroke cycle, because each piston goes up and down its cylinder twice during the sequence. One valve opens to let air into the cylinder. Another opens to let exhaust gases out. The fuel is sprayed into the cylinder by a fuel injector.

Fuel injector

Piston

Timing
The valves must open and close at the right time, and the fuel must be injected at the right moment. The camshaft (see opposite) is turned by a belt from the crankshaft (above).

Intake stroke
Piston moves down.
Air sucked into cylinder.

Compression stroke
Piston moves up.
Air squeezed into top of cylinder, making it hot.

Camshafts and valves

Valves are holes in the top of a cylinder that can be open or closed. The intake valve opens during the intake stroke to let in air. The exhaust valve opens during the exhaust stroke to let exhaust gases out. The valves are opened by the cams on the spinning camshaft. They are closed again by springs.

Camshaft

Spring

Valves

TECH FACT

In a diesel engine, the fuel ignites, or begins to burn, because the air in the cylinder is very hot. The air is hot because it is squeezed, or compressed, by the piston into a tiny space. This is why a diesel engine is also called a compression-ignition engine.

Power stroke
Fuel injected and explodes. Piston pushed down.

Exhaust stroke
Piston moves up. Exhaust gases pushed out.

Fuel and exhaust

A truck engine needs fuel to work. The fuel is stored in the fuel tank and burns in the cylinders. The fuel system moves the fuel from the tank to the cylinders in the engine. The system also supplies air to the engine, because the fuel cannot burn without air. The exhaust system removes waste gases left after the fuel burns.

Catalytic converter

Exhaust manifold

Air filters

A truck engine needs a lot of clean air in which to burn fuel. The air is sucked in from outside the truck through an air filter, which removes dirt from the air. Any dirt in the air would quickly clog up the engine's parts. There is a can-shaped air filter on the side of this truck.

TECH FACT

The exhaust gases flow along pipes to a box called a catalytic converter. There are special chemicals, called catalysts, inside the catalytic converter. These chemicals change harmful gases into less harmful gases. The new gases continue to travel along the exhaust pipe and out into the atmosphere.

The silencer

Blasts of exhaust gases travel along the exhaust pipe from the engine. The silencer muffles the blasts. This stops the gases coming out of the exhaust pipe with a loud bang.

Turbocharging

The more air an engine can get into its cylinders, the more fuel it can burn, and so the more power it can produce. Large truck engines have a device called a turbocharger (or just "turbo"). The turbo pumps air into the engine's cylinders, which makes the engine more powerful. The turbocharger is powered by exhaust gases coming from the cylinders.

Silencer

Exhaust pipe

Fuel tank

Turbocharger

Air intake

Cooling the engine

As an engine works, heat is made by the burning fuel and when the engine parts rub together. This makes parts of the engine very hot. They must be cooled to stop them getting too hot, which would make the engine seize up. The cooling system removes heat from the engine. It pumps water through the engine, which carries the heat away.

Pumping water

Water is pumped through spaces called ducts inside the engine block. The heat from the engine parts is transferred into the water. This cools the engine and heats up the water. The hot water then flows through the radiator, which cools it down again.

Radiator

Coolant hoses

Cooling water

The radiator is at the front of the truck. When the truck is moving, air flows over the radiator, cooling the water inside. When the truck is stationary, a fan blows air over the radiator.

TECH FACT

The cooling system is controlled by a device called a thermostat. When the engine temperature goes up, the thermostat detects the extra heat and turns on the water pump. This pumps water to the engine, cooling it again. Another thermostat controls the radiator cooling fan.

Intercooling

Some trucks have a device called an intercooler attached to the engine. Air from the turbocharger flows into the intercooler. The intercooler cools down the air. This makes the air more dense, which means that the same amount of air takes up less space. More air goes into the cylinders, which allows more fuel to be burned, giving the engine extra power.

Truck transmission

A truck's transmission connects the engine to the wheels. Its main part is the gearbox, which is used to change gears. A large truck may have 12 or more gears. Low gears are used for starting and driving at low speeds. High gears are used for driving at faster speeds.

Driveshafts and axles

Driveshafts are rods that go from the gearbox to the wheels. The gearbox spins the driveshafts and the driveshafts turn the wheels. An axle is a driveshaft that powers two wheels on opposite sides of a truck. The cogs that turn an axle are called a differential.

Axle

TECH FACT

Trucks that pull very heavy loads or work on rough ground need to travel at very low speeds. To do this, they have extra gears in each wheel hub. The gears make the wheels turn more slowly than the driveshaft. This system is called hub reduction.

Inside the gearbox

The gearbox allows the engine to turn the driveshafts at different speeds. The box is full of cogs of different sizes. Moving the stick shift makes different cogs interlock with each other. Each different combination of cogs is called a gear.

The clutch, gearbox, and driveshafts

The transmission contains the clutch, the gearbox, and the driveshafts. The engine has to be disconnected from the gearbox before the gears can be changed using the stick shift. This is done by the clutch. The gearbox turns the driveshafts at different speeds. The driveshafts turn the wheels.

Stick shift

i-TEC

Gearbox

Gearbox

Steering and brakes

A truck driver controls a truck with a steering wheel, pedals for the brakes, clutch, and accelerator, and the stick shift. The steering wheel makes the front wheel turn from side to side. Trucks have power steering to help the driver turn the wheels. The brakes slow the truck by stopping the wheels turning.

Discs and pads
There is a brake behind each wheel of a truck. A metal brake disc is connected to the driveshaft or axle. The disc turns with the wheel. When the driver presses the brake pedal, two pads squeeze the disc, which slows the wheel.

Air lines
Trailers have brakes, too. They are worked by air from the tractor unit. The air travels along air lines, or cables, which are connected when the trailer is attached to the tractor unit.

TECH FACT

Many trucks that are not articulated do not just have simple front-wheel steering. Heavy construction trucks, such as mobile cranes, have two sets of wheels at the front, and both sets do the steering. Some trucks use rear-wheel steering to turn around sharp bends.

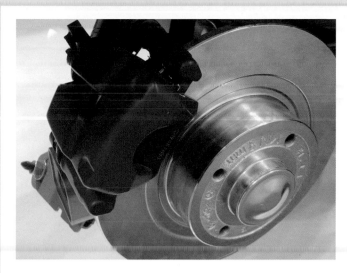

Air and hydraulics

Truck brakes are usually hydraulic. Hydraulic brakes use fluid to squeeze the brake pads together. Each brake has one or more brake cylinders with pistons inside. When the driver pushes the brake pedal, fluid is pushed into the cylinders. This pushes the piston, which pushes the pads onto the disc, stopping the wheel

Brake disc

Wheel bolt

Brake pads

Wheel hub

Safety and comfort

A modern truck uses the latest technology to make it as safe as possible to drive. There are also features that protect car drivers, who are risk serious injury in an accident with a large truck. Truck drivers spend many hours in their cabs every day, so it is important for them to be comfortable. They have fully adjustable seats and air-conditioned cabs.

Seat belts and air bags
Safety features in the cab include seat belts and air bags. A seat belt holds the driver in the driving seat during an accident. Air bags inflate instantly in an accident. They stop the driver from hitting the steering wheel or the sides of the cab.

Sleeper cabs
The biggest cabs are found on long-distance trucks. Their drivers can spend weeks on the road delivering their cargo. They have luxurious sleeper cabs, with a bed behind the seats, a washbasin, television, refrigerator, and plenty of storage space.

TECH FACT
In many countries, truck drivers are allowed to drive only for a certain number of hours a day. Drivers must take regular breaks for sleep, because driving while tired is dangerous. A device inside the cab called a tachograph (say TAKO–GRAAF) records when the truck is moving and when it is stopped.

Driver's seat

Microwave oven

Overhead storage

Refrigerator

Bed

Truck crash tests

New truck models are tested to see what happens to them in an accident. The results of the tests show how safe the truck is for the driver. Tests are also performed to see what happens if a car hits a truck. Bars on the chassis stop the car from going under the truck.

Special trucks

Many types of truck are designed to perform special jobs, from fighting fires and collecting trash, to racing around tracks and jumping over obstacles. These trucks usually have the same rigid chassis and cab as a cargo truck. The chassis and cab are built by a truck manufacturer, then a body is added to the chassis by a specialist truck maker.

Forklift trucks

Forklift trucks (see opposite page) raise heavy loads onto high places. A fork slides underneath the load and supports its weight. The fork is attached to a carriage. The carriage is moved up and down a vertical mast using a hydraulic system.

TECH FACT

Specialized trucks often have machinery on-board. For example, a dump truck has a lifting body, a garbage truck has a crusher, and a fire engine has a water tank and hoses. The machinery is operated by compressed air or hydraulics, and is powered by the truck's engine.

Concrete mixers

A concrete mixer carries wet concrete from a concrete plant to a building site. It mixes the ingredients together in its rotating drum. The drum spins backward to make the concrete come out and down a delivery chute.

Carriage

Fork

Hydraulic cylinder

Mast

Monster trucks
Truck enthusiasts convert normal pickup trucks into custom trucks by adding specialized parts. Monster trucks are custom trucks with high suspensions and giant tires used to squash scrap cars.

Cab

Glossary

Accelerate
To speed up.

Articulated truck
A truck that bends in the middle, made up of a tractor unit that tows a trailer.

Chassis
The main structure of a truck, usually made up of two strong rails. It supports all the other parts of the truck.

Cog
A wheel with teeth around its edge.

Component
An object that is part of a larger, more complex machine.

Compressor
A machine that squeezes (compresses) air into a smaller space.

Cylinder
A space inside an engine where fuel burns.

Diesel engine
An engine that uses diesel (sometimes called DERV) as its fuel.

Exhaust
The parts of a truck that carry waste gases away from the engine.

Filter
A device that removes pieces of dirt from a liquid or a gas.

Fuel system
The parts of a truck that store fuel and pump it to the engine's cylinders.

Hub
The central part of a wheel, where it is attached to the truck.

Hydraulic
Describes a machine that has parts moved by liquid pumped along pipes.

Piston
Part of an engine that slides up and down a cylinder.

Pressure
The push made by air inside a tire, or by gases inside an engine's cylinders.

Rigid truck
A truck that is not articulated. The chassis supports both the cab and the body.

Shock absorber
Part of a suspension that stops the suspension spring from becoming too squashed or stretched.

Skid
When a truck slides along the road without one or more of the wheels turning. It happens when the tires lose their grip on the road.

Suspension
Part of a truck that allows the wheels to move up and down as the truck goes over bumps.

Tractor unit
The front part of an articulated truck, which contains the driver's cab and the engine.

Trailer
The rear part of an articulated truck, which is towed by a tractor unit.

Valve
Part of an engine that opens temporarily to let fuel into a cylinder, or exhaust gases out.

Further reading

The Need for Speed: Monster Trucks
by Michael Johnstone
(Topeka Bindery, 2002)

World Encyclopedia of Trucks
by Peter J Davies
(Southwater, 2007)

World's Greatest Trucks and Earth Movers
by Ian Graham
(Raintree, 2005)

Web Sites

Due to the changing nature of Internet links, PowerKids Press has developed an online list of Web sites related to the subject of this book. This site is updated regularly. Please use this link to access this list:
www.powerkidslinks.com/mio/trucks

Index